C.I.U.

Children's Intelligence Unit
SAVES LONDON

AGENT T

AGENT G

AGENT V

AGENT L

AGY LOUKAIDES

AuthorHouse™ UK
1663 Liberty Drive
Bloomington, IN 47403 USA
www.authorhouse.co.uk
UK TFN: 0800 0148641 (Toll Free inside the UK)
UK Local: 02036 956322 (+44 20 3695 6322 from outside the UK)

Because of the dynamic nature of the Internet, any web addresses or links contained
in this book may have changed since publication and may no longer be valid. The views
expressed in this work are solely those of the author and do not necessarily reflect the
views of the publisher, and the publisher hereby disclaims any responsibility for them.

Any people depicted in stock imagery provided by Getty Images are models,
and such images are being used for illustrative purposes only.
Certain stock imagery © Getty Images.

This book is printed on acid-free paper.

ISBN: 978-1-6655-9707-4 (sc)
ISBN: 978-1-6655-9708-1 (e)

Print information available on the last page.

Published by AuthorHouse 03/14/2022

authorHOUSE

CHAPTER 1

It was just another busy day across the noisy mixed kebab metropolis of London when suddenly an important News flash crossed our waves...

'Hi, I'm an important'

'NEWSFLASH!'

"Evening, this is Trisha News, reports are coming in that London is under attack! Monster Mike is running wild, destroying all in his path and terrorising residents, as he works his way through our great city"

AAAAAAAAAAAAAAAAAHHHHHHHHHHHHHHHHHH!

(From all the extras)

"Authorities advice all to stay indoors and not to approach him as he is very big, very green, very bored and only slightly hungry as he is on a new low diet!"

"We have repelled the Vikings, Romans and
COVID but this former resident nemesis of
Edmonton has the city at his mercy…

From her Majesty's Government, please C.I.U….we need you!!"

"The weather will follow next."

CHAPTER 2

Meanwhile back at the C.I.U top secret base
in happy go likey North London........

The gang where just chilling and practising their skills.....

"Look gang, if I mix my cola with explosive
M&M's look what happens..........."

Said a very sweaty and hesitant Agent T, then
suddenly the base was shaken by a blinding flash
and deafing bang that filled the high tech room

KERPOWWWWWWWWWWWWWWWW!!

After the dust and noise had settled down, a very
torn up and splattered Agent T broke the silence

"Wow!! It gives you one great boost....
once I get the formula, right?"

"Agent T you are silly ya ya ya........ sorry guys, ya
ya,that strange language keeps coming out of in
my sentences, it must have been a, ya ya, baby
thing from the past" said a confused Agent G

"I know Agent G all those bang bangs is putting me off my
exercise's, you have made me drop enough trolleys in the
supermarket in the past Agent T" said a very annoyed Agent V

Agent T suddenly started to cough very
loudly in a beat box rhythm

"I need some water please Agent G"

Said a gasping Agent T

Within a split second WOOOOOOOOOOOOOSSSSHHH! Agent
G was a blur clasping a glass of water, "Here you go" she
said with an expression of achivement. "Blimey that was
quick Agent G" said Agent T with an impressive grin."Quick......
you must be joking, I'm having an off day?" said Agent G

"I'm tired now after lifting those fridges and all those bang
bangs, I'm going to crash down now on that brand new
chair in the corner?" said a very exhausted Agent V

**Once Agent V jumped onto the big shiny new red chair
that was inviting him to park there and was only just
delivered that morning from Argos...you hear.......**

"Ooooooooooooooooiiiiiiiii, do you mind!!" said the chair.
"Sorry Agent L, I didn't know you was in camouflage
ha! Ha!" said Agent V scratching his head and
wondering how she manged to pull that off.

"That's ok Agent V I'm just revising my Ikea project,
pretty impressive or what" said a very proud Agent L

**Then suddenly the laughter was broken
by a radio annousement .....**

'THIS IS LONDON CALLING!'

"Agent T, Agent G, Agent V and Agent L the country needs you, your training is to be cut short as Monster Mike is creating havoc in good old London town...his munching everything in his path because the bookies is closed! We will send over Sgt king - Pin at 0800 hours to collect you and take you to your mentor, the retired Bond, for a summary of the situation and don't worry your mummy's and daddy's have given us permission, good luck as we are depending on you...over and out!"

"Blimey this is it gang........... we are going in" Said Agent T "At last. ...No more fridges" said an excited Agent V. "Shame I was just going to turn into a .... Bed" said very disappointed Agent L

The gang are ready, the situation is ready ....the adventure is ready, I know it's rather exciting!

CHAPTER 3

The early pease and quiet morning was interrupted by the roar of screeching tyres and a loud air horn, it was Sgt King - Pin on time to pick up the C.I.U foursome

"Mini cab!!" He said while slamming on the brakes of his jeep and chewing on a stick of 'what's this' Said the experienced Sgt King- Pin

"horrrrrrrrrrray our lift is here!"

yelled the excited C.I.U Agents

"Welcome Sgt King-Pin, we were expecting you, do you know the way to the secret base of the retired Bond?

"Well I do but I did bring the sat nav just in case because.........Don't forget I'm only a cat you know"

The team all bundled into the mini cab, oops I meant Army jeep with all their equipment, as it went like the clappers to the top-secret base of the retired Bond!

"Move over, get your arm off me head, mind your knee, who let one go?"

It was a bit of a tight squeeze!

CHAPTER 4

Sgt King -Pin raced the C.I.U Agents to the
retired Bond's hideout in deepest Crouch end

BRRRRRRRRRRRRRRRRRMMMMMMMMMMMM!

'I just haven't met you yet...........la la la!'

"Wicked singalong Sgt King - Pin" yelled the C.I.U team

I was introduced to it by the retired Bond when I was
just a nipper, I think it's a guy called Michael bubble or
something like that.......my memory isn't what it used to
be, sometimes I think I'm a 'Tush Tush' I think it was
a nick name that my former landlady gave me?"

As the car raced through deepest darkest crouch End...
It finally arrived at the retired Bonds hideout...

The team all spilled out and where immediately
greeted by the sentry on duty..

"HALT! Who goes there?" shouted out
the alert guardsman on duty

"Relax soldier we are C.I.U come to see the retired
Bond, your good soldier what's your name and rank?"

Said Agent T in a proud way

"Private Lucozade, number 999 sir yes sir ok Sir" "Ok soldier you do go on a bit" said a weird looking Agent G

"Agent T, he half looks like your dad and why is he in a uniform that is little to big for him? Said Agent V looking the soldier up and down

"Well Agent V it is, but keep it quiet, he told me the oversized uniform is good to carry vital supplies like beer, beer and...... more beer?"

"There is the retired Bond.........I'll have to change back to normal for him" said Agent L dressed up like a mailbox

"I was expecting you C.I.U"

said the slightly worn and eldely tall figure dressed in his Tuxedo Jim Jams . "Now let's get on with business so pay attention as I must open a supermarket later for the council as I have been in big demand since I hanged up my '00' status, they were the good old days. DC was my understudy during the war, he is doing well but was never as good as me, ask all those housewives?"

"Monster Mic, was spotted on a night out at Ladbrokes uttering the words, what happened to my dosh?"

"He Is running wild in London and is not a happy green bunny, you know the score the usual 'I will take over the world' routine a bit like Simon Cowell, your job team is simples......STOP HIM!"

There was collective ' woooooooooooooow!!' from the team

"Now off you go and don't forget you are the little spies
that everyone loves so it is going to be a 'Goldfinger'
for all and 'Let's live and let die' for her 'Majesty
service'.... I know I do go on a bit ? Good luck team"

The team quickly got back into Sgt King -Pin's jeep
and speed off into the night to nail Monster Mike and
rescue London, it was once again a bit of a tight fit..

"Get you knee out of my face, who's foot
is that, who let one go again?"

CHAPTER 5

As the C.I.U team race across the country trying to stop Monster Mike, unknown to them Monster Mike has got wind of their rescue attempt and trust me he has a lot of wind?

"This is the boss speaking Bernie,oops I mean Ninja B, as I have just heard C.I.U are on my tail and may I say it's a rather nice tail especially for my age, so I want you to EXTEMINATE THEM the Potters Bar way then get the Vodka on ice, I do like my little tibble?"

"OK Mr Boss and wait to I get you home for talking to me like that in this book"

As C.I.U where singing away to SGT King - Pins all-time cat greatest hits they suddenly realise they are being followed

"Blimy! gang we are being followed by a Asian woman dressed in ninja gear and mishandling her helicopter" **said Agent V**

"She not a good driver is she" **said Agent G**

"yep, she should have bought a Range Rover instead, said **Agent L**

"Let's get ready to have a rumble gang "said **Agent T**

"Right C.I.U you will be extmi....extm........What's that flash word the Boss said, blimey I forgot, stuff it…. you will be flattened!" **yelled Ninja B**

"Right agents let's go, Agent V get out and pick up our car, Ninja G push him as fast as you can go and Agent L turn into a Bomb but make sure you don't get blown up for good as we still need you" **ordered Agent T**

"Will this do Agent T"

"Great...........aim at that helicopter, concentrate and jump up like it's your last sweet in the world" **Said agent T**

"Ok, here we go........bounce higher and higher, I hope the last one is a chocolate one" **Grinned Agent L**

With one last all mighty effort, Agent L hit her target

KAAAAAAAAAAAAAAPPPPOWWWWW!!

"ooonowwwwwwwwwwww they got me, I have to go back to Potters Bar now and explain all, pesky C.I.U" **cried Ninja B as she floated off**

'Hooooooooooooooooooooooooorrrrrayyyy!'

Yelled the fabulous foursome as they carried on to take on Monster Mike who knows they are coming and is waiting for them?

CHAPTER 6

As C.I.U are fast approaching London, the crowds start
to gather as Monster Mike is in the background......
just munching away on anything he could find

'Munch! Munch! Munch!

"Hi to all, this Trisha News reporting live in old London
town reporting on the oncoming battle between Monster
Mike and C.I.U Team as the mixed residents of this great
Chinese owned city gather to witness this all mighty
punch -up, early I asked a few people what they think
of C.I.U taking on this Edmonton based Monster"

Ms D

"I'm so happy the little agents are on their
way, he, she or whatever will be good for us
all, praise the lord and all at Tesco's"

Ms P

"Don't call me madame, its Ms,I think it is great for us and my
puggsy for C.I.U to rescue us it was never like this in Vegas

Ms L

"Well. I think at least they can try and keep the
noise down a bit as I have a terrible headache"

N & M

"Man this is bigger than Elvis, go Team C.I.U"

Mr Frilly

"Man can you imagine the prices after all has
settled down on property around here, there
is always few pennies in punch ups?"

"Well public, let's hope all ends well for gallant Agents
but if doesn't, I can be booked for anything, and I
mean anything, this is Trisha News for Hot News.

CHAPTER 7

The C.I.U team approached a very knackered London as
Sgt king -Pin slammed on the breaks in Westminster

"We are here "**Cried the Sgt.**

The team eyeballed the battered city with rumble and
destruction everywhere, a bit like their bedrooms?

"Blimey, there mums will be unhappy with
this, can you imagine the size of the mop you'll
need to sort this out" **Said Agent L**

**Then suddenly the silence was broken
by the growl of Monster Mike**

"GROOOOOOOOOOWWWWLLLL!,

I have to give up the fags it's killing my growl!"
said the menacing, hungry Monster

He looked down on our young heroes and growled again

"I have been expecting you little ones, are you ready to meet
that big Toys R us in the sky" **he said in a cockney mean way**

The team all stood back in a defensive way,

"We are Lucky we have Sgt king-
pin for back- up" **said Agent T**

"Sgt King-pin, Sgt king-Pin where are you going?"

"Stuff this, his big and green and he doesn't like cats dressed as an action man, I don't want to hang about I have cat things to do because don't forget I'm only a cat you know?"

and with that Sgt King pin disappeared in the car as fast as if it was his last 'What's this'

"That's great, we need some serious back-up now or we are disposable nappies for Monster Mike" **said Agent G**

Just at that moment the sky was broken by the scream of jet engines

"Red leader, Red leader Captain P to the rescue, homing in on that green slime" **yelled the pilot**

"Hooray!! it the best fighter pilot in the world, and sponsored by Playstation. He is the most decorated fighter ever, he is undefeated and his going in for the kill.... his coming in, he will get us out of trouble, his coming, his coming" **said Agent V**

"Typical, just when I was enjoying my role, never mind let's give him a taste of ...... Charcoal" **said a menacing Monster Mike**

And with those words Monster Mic released a flory of charcoal rockets at Captain P which hit their target in a very BK way...

KABOOOOOOOOOOOOOOOMMMM!!

"Blimey! That's great, here he comes....there he goes, right it's up to us now team" **said Agent T**

And with that the team run into the rumble of what was Westminster cathedral for all mighty final punch - Up' chased by Monster Mike

"I wish they stay still; I'm getting on a bit for all this running around" **said the out of Breath Monster Mike.**

CHAPTER 8

In the busted doggy smelling Cathedral C.I.U where cornered off by Monster Mike

"Right C.I.U, you are odds on for a massacre, or 10 to 1 for a draw or evens to lose in extra time either way you will lose and why I'm I talking in the ancient language of .... LADBROKES?" **said the confused but vicious green menace**

"It's time to kick in like the retired Bond" **said Agent T**

"It's live or let die" **he added**

"Yep,it's time for him to get his Goldfinger right where it hurts" **said Agent L**

"It's Tomorrow Never Dies for us" **said Agent V**

"Let him have it in his Moonraker" **said agent G**

"Why we all talking Bond" **they all said together confused**

"Ok Agents lets go go go........Agent V lift up that heavy elastic from the floor, Agent G as fast as you can get me some Sentex from the cellar and Agent L turn into a big shiny mmmmmmmmm...boxing glove and I'll set up the charge on you, we only get one shot....so let's make it count, this is it Agents operation KNOCK OUT" yelled Agent T

"Now Agent V pull the elastic back, Agent
G aim Agent L at Monster Mike

Now let's deliver the knockout blow for this
misrable looking monster, now on the count of
three let him have it" **yelled out Agent** T

"Is that it,is that all you little ones can do, I'm
going to enjoy wiping you Agents out" **said Monster
Mike as he started to bre**ak into laughter

1. **Agent V grip the elastic**
2. **Agent G take aim**
3. **Agent L load up the knockout blow**

"Now let go"

So, with one almighty effort the Agents let go and........

KAPPPPPPPOOOWW!
BOOOOOOOOOOMMMMM!
WAAAAAAAAAAAALLLOPP!

**It was direct hit right on Monster Mike's nose that
sent him back to his local area with him crying out...**

"I don't want to play anymore it's made me
all purple, where's my mummy?"

"One Nil to the C.I.U, one Nil to the C.I.U, let's all
go home for tea and sweets, we are still kids you know"

they all shouted.

CHAPTER 9

Soon the whole of London heard of the daring win by C.I.U against Monster Mike and before you could say, sticky sherbet it went worldwide.....

EXCLUSIVE NEWS

"Hi this is Trisha News reporting from Bucks Palace on the presentation of the biggest bravery award ever given to Agents by Queen Liz..........now are we off air as I have to take these shoes off as they are killing my feet"

Meanwhile inside Bucks Palace......

"I give you the medals for the bestest thing any small Agents have done for me and Phil.....and, all most forgot, the rest of the country ever, well done to all"

"Cheers sweetheart" **said a very proud Agent T**

"Thank you you,r Majesty, did I say that right now can I go back and lift fridges?" **said an egar Agent V**

"Thanks you but I do prefer it in purple or even pink?" **said a fashionable Agent G**

But hang on a moment ...where is Agent L ...

"Sorry gang but I couldn't help it" **said the shiny Goldy Throne,** "shall I turn back now"

"Ha, Ha, Ha! Giggle, Giggle, Giggle!"

roared the C.I.U team

THE END

.....or is it?

Printed in the United States
by Baker & Taylor Publisher Services